Acting Edition

THE MOST MASSIVE WOMAN WINS

BY MADELEINE GEORGE

THE MOST MASSIVE WOMAN WINS
Copyright © 2009, Madeleine George

All Rights Reserved

ISBN 978-1-6238-4135-5
www.playscripts.com
www.concordtheatricals.com

MUSIC AND THIRD-PARTY MATERIALS USE NOTE

Licensees are solely responsible for obtaining formal written permission from copyright owners to use copyrighted music and/or other copyrighted third-party materials (e.g. artworks, logos) in the performance of this play and are strongly cautioned to do so. If no such permission is obtained by the licensee, then the licensee must use only original music and materials that the licensee owns and controls. Licensees are solely responsible and liable for clearances of all third-party copyrighted materials, including without limitation music, and shall indemnify the copyright owners of the play(s) and their licensing agent, Dramatists Play Service, an imprint of Concord Theatricals Corp., against any costs, expenses, losses and liabilities arising from the use of such copyrighted third-party materials by licensees. For music, please contact the appropriate music licensing authority in your territory for the rights to any incidental music.

IMPORTANT BILLING AND CREDIT REQUIREMENTS

If you have obtained performance rights to this title, please refer to your licensing agreement for important billing and credit requirements.

Cast of Characters

CARLY, 31 years old. In acid washed jeans, a rhinestone-studded denim jacket and a sweatshirt with high-top Reebok sneakers.

CEL, 26 years old. In a long dress. Her name is pronounced "Seel," it's short for Celia.

SABINE, 25 years old. In à la mode nineties officewear.

RENNIE, 17 years old. In overalls and a flannel. She is a high-school senior.

Scene

The play takes place in a liposuction clinic waiting room.

Time

1990s.

General Notes

—All four women do not have to be overweight.

—Rennie is the only bulimic.

—It is important that the play be established as humorous from the outset.

—A great deal of the 'dialogue' is directed out to the audience; the women are often able to pick up on each others' thoughts without speaking straight at one another.

—The chants are genuine hopscotch, jump rope and hand-clap rhymes from my own childhood.

—We used blocking inspired by children's games: London Bridge and Mulberry Bush for the scoliosis check, Red Rover for the thesis defense, Musical Chairs for Carly's job interviews.

Monologue Notes

—Each monologue is delivered out to the audience.

—The three women not speaking at any one time should not look at the speaker, but some way should be found to indicate that they are listening—stomps, thigh slaps, or claps that punctuate moments of tension or anger, for example. In the 'dance, run, jump, fly' sequence at the end of Cel's monologue the other three women did a slow flap of their arms, reprising the bird movement from earlier in the play. At that point they also turned to look at Cel.

—Carly talks really fast and never gets sentimental, but she loves her kid.

—Sabine is extremely hard on herself and never gives herself a break; instead of getting sad she always gets angry, right through to the very last line.

—Rennie is perpetually panicked and jumpy; it's as if there's nothing holding her down to the floor. She laughs a lot to disguise her fear.

—Cel is not crazy. Her monologue is driven by her own need to tell her story. She does not relive the moment of her self-immolation, she tells us about it (this is important). Realization and catharsis come at the very end of the monologue, not before.

Acknowledgments

The Most Massive Woman Wins premiered at the Public Theater in New York City as part of the Young Playwrights Festival in October 1994. It was directed by Phyllis S. K. Look; the set design was by Allen Moyer; the costume design was by Karen Perry; the lighting design was by Pat Dignan; the production stage manager was Elise-Ann Konstantin; and the dramaturg was Sarah Higgins. The cast was as follows:

SABINE	Candace Taylor
CARLY	Amy Ryder
RENNIE	Elaina Davis
CEL	Suzanne Costallos

THE MOST MASSIVE WOMAN WINS
by Madeleine George

(Setting: Waiting room of a liposuction clinic, furnished with four chairs.)

(At rise: The light is bright and sterile.)

(SABINE, CEL, CARLY, and RENNIE are seated on the chairs. For several minutes they stare at their magazines, fidget, cough, cross and recross their legs and flip magazine pages in an otherwordly, choreographed little dance.)

RENNIE. I'm about to have my body surgically removed.

CEL. (CEL's *chant runs underneath the others' comments:*) Cinderella dressed in yella…

RENNIE. They're taking stuff out—big chunks, sloppy hunks.

CEL. Went to the ball to meet her fella…

SABINE. I'm here for the ass and inner thigh combo.

CEL. On the way her girdle busted…

CARLY. He said my butt and my gut is the parts he would pay for.

CEL. How many people were disgusted?

CARLY. Aw, shit, I hate waiting. If I'm gonna do this I just wanna do it, you know?

RENNIE. Scared?

CARLY. It's not that…

RENNIE. If you're here you're here because you want to be here.

ALL. On the way her girdle busted
How many people were disgusted?

RENNIE. One—

SABINE. Two—

CEL. Three—

CARLY. Four—

ALL. *(Addressing the audience:)* Five—

CARLY. The other night my boyfriend goes to me, he's spread eagle on the couch giving his gut some air watching Monday Night Football and during the commercial he goes, "We don't have steak anymore. How come is it we never have steak?" I'm about to say, "You want steak, buy steak. Take it out a your paycheck, if you want steak so bad," but then he says to me, like, right in the same breath he goes, "What am I saying? You're too fat for steak. Last thing you need is fatty red meat." Just like that, then he tips back his beer and the conversation's over.

SABINE. What did you say to him?

CARLY. I don't know, nothing. It's like I can't tell him off. Then later he leaves me this liposuction ad he clipped from the classifieds on my bedside table with a signed blank check. Is the guy subtle or what?

SABINE. Shit…

CARLY. You think it doesn't make me sick? What's the matter with me that I can't tell Frank Nowak where to stick it? I'm a weenie, that's what. A big fat wimp. How am I supposed to look my own kid in the face?

ALL. My boyfriend gave me peaches
My boyfriend gave me pears
My boyfriend gave me fifty cents
and kicked me down the stairs!

CARLY. C'ai play too?

RENNIE. She's too *fat* for jump rope.

CARLY. That feeling, you know it, it's the one you've been getting since you were six years old.

ALL. Miss Suzy had a baby
She named her Mary Lynn
She put her in the bathtub
Just to see if she could swim
She drank up all the water

She ate up all the soap
She tried to eat the bathtub but it wouldn't go down her throat!

CARLY. It starts like a tidal wave under your feet and grows and grows until you forget your name and the people you love and all you know is you have to eat.

CEL. You think if you dared to open your mouth all of creation would get sucked right in.

SABINE. You think about eating alone in your bed, making love to a Twinkie, devouring it desperately, HUNGry for it.

CARLY. You sneak out of bed, you don't think he hears you, you run down the stairs to where you hid the Sugar Smacks behind the TV, you're alone at last and you're eating great fistfuls, hand over hand. It tastes like everything you never had.

SABINE. It rises from a moan to a wail in your ears, it's pulsing through your body, it's chocolate you're hearing. It's the middle of the night and there's a winter storm warning you're about to drive across town for a 52 ounce bar of Toblerone love.

RENNIE. Now you're gorging, cramming it thick down your throat, all Chewy Chips Ahoy and no room to breathe, you have to you have to you have to have it, then you're doubling over, spitting and shaking, face in the toilet, so sorry, so ashamed.

CARLY. You eat and you eat until you can't fit another bite into your body, you're bloated, drowned from the inside out.

SABINE. A beached whale, you can't move an inch.

CEL. You're done.

SABINE. You're done for.

RENNIE. So you throw out the evidence. Flush down the rest.

SABINE. Regain control.

CARLY. And you go back to doing what you were doing before.

> *(They reprise the waiting dance.)*

SABINE. But you know you did it.

RENNIE. You may be making like everything is fine fine fine but you know what you've done, you bit it, you blew it.

CARLY. It's your fuckin fault—you lost control.

CEL. You know better than that.

SABINE. So it's time to make an adult decision.

CARLY. *(Smacks her own butt.)* Throw out the evidence.

RENNIE. You think of every sin in your past—

CEL. Every slice of pie—

CARLY. Every french fry—

SABINE. Every chocolate croissant—

RENNIE. You know it's all in there, simmering under your skin, and this nice man is gonna get rid of it all. Purify you.

ALL. Clean slate.

RENNIE. The ultimate purge.

SABINE. You are responsible for your own behaviour.

ALL. You are responsible.

RENNIE. You are guilty.

> *(Lights shifts, a whistle is blown.)*

CEL. *(Bellowing:)* Scoliosis check!

> *(CARLY, RENNIE, and SABINE scramble into position down center.)*

CEL. Shirts off!

CARLY. *(To RENNIE:)* She's such a fatso.

RENNIE. *(To CARLY:)* She weighs a hundred and four, I peeked at the scale.

CARLY. *(To RENNIE:)* Oh gross, look, she's getting boobs.

CEL. Bend at the waist!

CARLY. If you get them early it means you're a slut.

CEL. Rotate to face me!

RENNIE. I hope I don't get them.

CEL. Touch your hands to the floor!

CARLY. It's her fault cause she always eats two desserts at lunch.

CEL. Rotate again!

CARLY. We'll never get them like she's got them.

CEL. Stand up!

RENNIE. We'll never be so disgusting as her.

    (Lights shift, a whistle is blown.)

SABINE. Look who's not playing.

CEL. *(Sassy:)* She's excused.

CARLY. She's always excused. Bitch.

CEL. She can't play dodgeball, she's ginormous!

SABINE. Gigundo!

CARLY. Gigantoid!

CEL. *(Yelling to* RENNIE:*)* Hey fatso, what position are YOU playing, huh?

RENNIE. *(Quietly:)* Offense.

    (Lights shift, a whistle is blown, they scramble into a new formation.)

SABINE. *(Announcing:)* In defense of my thesis: "Images of Women in Cold War and Post-Cold War Era Media Colon Self-Denial and Self-Esteem."

(Confidently:) I refer you once again to both Kruger and Wolf as well as to Baudrillard's discussion of the hypnotizing image.

(She takes a deep breath, then speaks quickly:)

In conclusion I would like to emphasize my belief that this and re-
lated subject matters are pertinent, if not crucial, to our postmodern
society. Although inquiry into such subjects is somewhat scarce in
journals today, I predict that as the information age hits its stride,
and as feminist thought becomes more seamlessly integrated into
mainstream American consciousness, we will see a proliferation of
influential and powerful work concerning the subjugation of wom-
en's bodies through media images. Thank you.

RENNIE. Ms...Rowe... Can you explain again ex-act-ly how this
subject is relevant? I can't see how this topic merits scholarly investi-
gation when it has such a minute effect on the population as a whole.

SABINE. If eating disorders are as prevalent among women as re-
cent studies show, and if women comprise as they do 52% of the
population I think you'll find this is quite a relevant subject for in-
vestigation—

CEL. *(Cutting in:)* I fail to understand why these women can't simply
"get over" disorders that you claim are caused by looking at two-
dimensional images.

SABINE. Obviously it's a bit more complicated than that—

CARLY. *(Cutting in:)* As every person is responsible for his own at-
titudes about himself, it should be a simple matter for a person to
alter his image of self, should it not?

SABINE. *(Stumbling over words:)* Once again I'd like to remind you
that studies show physical appearance, that is, conformity to soci-
etally established standards of beauty, has a much greater impact
on women's lives than on men's, this includes social status, marital
status, income and work-related achievements—

RENNIE. *(Cutting in:)* It seems to me you're getting a little emotional
about this. I can understand why—this hits a little close to home for
you. For that reason I would have advised you to choose a topic you
could remain somewhat objective about.

(Lights shift, whistle.)

CARLY. What about benefits?

RENNIE. *(Strongly emphasizing the 'Mizz':)* We haven't yet decided if this is an appropriate job for you, Ms.—

CARLY. Kinski.

RENNIE. Let's hold off our discussion of fine points and sundries until we are able to come to a full understanding.

CARLY. Sure thing, sir.

> *(Whistle.)*

SABINE. Let me be frank, Ms.—

CARLY. Kinski.

SABINE. I don't think you have fully considered the physical taxation that is put on a person in this line of work.

CARLY. Sir I been in food service all my life.

SABINE. The waitstaff here are part of our family. And because of the extreme demands placed on their persons I demand that every member of the family be in peak physical condition.

CARLY. Alls I'm saying sir is I can do this job and I just wanna know about the benefits you—

> *(Whistle.)*

CEL. *(Overlapping:)* I'm afraid I'm not fully getting through to you, Ms.—

CARLY. Kinski, Kinski.

CEL. Allow me to speak as plainly as possible. I really don't think the restaurant can use a woman of your—stature at this time. Please don't take this personally, but with the aesthetic atmosphere I am trying to cultivate there are certain, hmmm, discrepancies that cannot be tolerated.

CARLY. I been trying to tell you—

> *(Whistle.)*

RENNIE. *(Cutting in:)* Most of the girls I hire are eighteen, nineteen years old.

(Whistle.)

SABINE. They haven't been through what you've been through I'm sure.

(Whistle.)

CEL. I hope you won't be unduly upset by this.

(Whistle.)

RENNIE. Not everything can be fair in this world, I'm afraid.

(Lights shift, whistle is blown. During Cel's trial SABINE paces the perimeter of the stage calling off, RENNIE and CARLY become CEL's reflected image in the mirror.)

CEL. My husband has a theory. He's figured it out.

SABINE. Cel!

CEL. My husband says to me Cel, can't you see yourself in the mirror? I say Yeah.

SABINE. Cel!

CEL. He says so why don't you do something about it, it's for your own good he says. You know about the heart failure and the brain tumors and amputations, but how many times I have to tell you what really happens to girls who get too big—

SABINE. Celia!

CEL. *(Bitter, completing the quote:)* —honey.

SABINE. *(Calling for her:)* Honey?

CEL. He says fat girls go crazy more than thin girls do.

SABINE. Goddamn it girl, where did you get to now?

CEL. It has to do with metabolism, he says, he read it in the encyclopedia, because fat girls let their cells get unbalanced.

SABINE. Ce-lie, it's freezing in here!

CEL. See your body has to send more blood down to the fat so it can't spend the time that it should in your brain. It's like there's this system inside you and everything in it has to balance, if you add a little too much of one thing you throw off the rest.

> *(The mirror reflections begin to flap their arms like birds, then turn away from CEL, released.)*

SABINE. For Christ's sake, Cel, what is going **on** here in the middle of November? Every window and door is swung out on its hinges, the place is a mess, there are *birds* flying by me in the goddamn kitchen, what's the matter with you, girl? What is wrong with you, woman?

CEL. *(Still to the audience:)* That's why he said maybe a surgical cure, so I can get rid of that parasite fat. I can maybe start acting more normal he says.

> *(Lights shift, final whistle is blown.)*

ALL. Little Baby Sally was sick in bed
Sally called for mama and her mama said
Little Baby Sally you're not sick
All you need is a peppermint stick.

> *(Lights shift, hospital gowns fly in, the women stand behind them and undress during the next exchange, then put the gowns on.)*

CARLY. My mama was—she used to say "plump and juicy."

RENNIE. My mother said for big girls like me it was ugly to let people see the stuff you were made of. Especially legs and shoulders and the inside of your mouth.

SABINE. Our mothers all taught us the same thing.

CARLY. Hush up, Carly girl.

SABINE. Sit still till we get to grandma's and mama'll give you a cookie.

CEL. If you're good you can lick the bowl.

CARLY. Do you kiss your mother with that mouth?

RENNIE. Sit up straight and eat only what you're offered.

SABINE. Children are starving in Denmark.

CEL. Eat your peas.

SABINE. Or was it Detroit?

CARLY. Open wide!

RENNIE. What's the matter, don't you feel well?

CARLY. What's wrong, don't you want dessert?

SABINE. Here, darling, have some of mama's home-baked cherry pie.

CEL. Chicken-fried steak.

RENNIE. Chocolate mousse.

> *(They all laugh and "mmm" in agreement.)*

CARLY. Baby, you are so be-yoo-tiful, just like a calendar girl with those big brown eyes and that beautiful skin!

RENNIE. Why did everyone always tell me I had beautiful skin?

CARLY. And babes, someday you'll thank me for letting you put on that extra padding. When your airplane crashes on the highest peak of the Himalayas all those skinny passengers are gonna starve to death seven ways till Sunday and you will survive for months and months, living only off what you have stored in your tush.

SABINE. Mama's always right. You just wait.

> *(RENNIE, CEL, and SABINE return to their corners to sit, lights up on CARLY in the center.)*

CARLY. No my mama was not always right. No, you shoulda seen her when he'd come home nights, the whole place'd get quiet like the grave, I swear, she'd be pussyfootin around him jumping like a sick kitten every time he made a move…all you could hear was him chewing with his mouth open and his silverware hitting the plastic plate.

It's too late for my mama, it's too late for me now. But the day my kid was born I made it a promise that she was gonna know who she was.

No one was gonna walk all over my kid. No one was gonna give her a goddamned blank check.

Then the other day I come home from work and there she is, my stupid kid, sitting on the bathroom floor, leaning against the tub, and her long blonde hair is dyed pitch black, I swear, black as tar, and it's dripping black rivers all down her face and her neck… I could have killed her right then and there, I wanted to knock her head off of her skinny little neck.

Instead of killing her I say, Jesus, Christ, what the hell did you do to your hair, and she's crying and choking and she goes, Ma! and points at the counter. I looked and I swear I thought I was going to toss my cookies. She has got one of these EPT plus pregnancy tests laid out there, you know, the little stick kind? Pink, pregnant, white, not pregnant…there's that little stick leaning up against the box it came in and the end is as bright pink as an Easter egg, pink as all fuck, pardon my French, pink like a baby's butt is pink. Talk about history repeating itself. Suddenly I'm sixteen again with that sinking feeling in my stomach looking at the little test tube, holding it up against the light bulb in the upstairs closet…

So I'm trying to figure out what exactly the black hair has got to do with the pink stick. I say, Is that or is that not an EPT plus pregnancy test? and she nods, so I say, Is that or is that not a pink stick you got there? and she says, It's pink. I say, So you're pregnant, so you dyed your hair black? She starts sobbing and wailing and she goes, I knew you wouldn't understand, you never understand anything about me! She bangs past me and stomps down the hall and slams the bedroom door behind her. I'm thinking, what's to understand? You're totally nuts!

I'm standing there alone in the bathroom. The place looks like a tornado hit, there's little bottles and vials and tubes all over, with that little pink baby-positive stick lying right in the middle like the eye of the hurricane, the evil eye, more like, still and pink and sticking its tongue out at me. Ha. You lost. You fucked up. I'm thinking, what happened? I thought only fat girls didn't know what they were doing. My kid's a beauty, gorgeous, skinny, tall, why the hell didn't she stand up for herself? How could she let this happen? She's got no goddam spine!

Then I'm back to the time when she was just two years old, the first time I saw her throw a tantrum. It was in the kitchen, over a purple popsicle. I was so surprised at the force inside her little body. She stamped her bare feet on the kitchen floor and balled up her fists and bared her tiny white teeth at me, and when I said, No, and shut the refrigerator door with the toe of my shoe she looked up into my face and squinted, she wasn't three feet tall, and her mouth got tiny like the…head of a nail, and I knew I had someone to contend with then.

So I go into the bedroom, sit down on the edge of the bed and pat her on the back. Stacey, sweets, hey, hey, it's alright. You gotta be strong and make your own choice, but whatever decision you want to make, I'm behind you, okay? We'll do whatever you choose. She stops sniffing. She breathes in and out. I say, So, listen, uh…have you talked to the guy about this yet? And she says, nasty, No, Ma, God. Boys don't like girls who boss them around.

(Lights down on CARLY, up on SABINE in her corner, during the course of the monologue she moves center.)

SABINE. Like my friend Michael. Michael and I, we are best friends. We go for sushi and foxtrot once a month at the full moon. The thing is, all our conversations go like this: Michael tells me about his love life, I support him. Michael whines about his girlfriend, I console him. Michael moans about the horrors of latex, I sympathize, I hug him, I make him tea, and recently I have found myself possessed with rage absolutely every time I lay eyes on him. Because I am so very tired of being everyone's warm and fuzzy sounding board. I want to be a full-blown sexual threat right now. I want to get down on my hands and knees and do it, sweaty, hot, savage, wrong, mor-ally rep-re-hensible… If my mother could hear me now…she wasn't out of her foundation garments long enough to have sex. I was an immaculate conception. My father stuck his tongue in her ear and bang, there I was, I appeared just like that on the kitchen counter in an attractive presentation basket. That's how we fat women do it, you know. We just close our eyes and think beautiful thoughts and our offspring arrive with the afternoon mail.

In undergrad psychology we learned about these people, they were called split-brain patients, and each hemisphere of their brain could work on a task without the other half knowing. In the films they showed us they taught this one guy to build blocks into towers with his left hand only. Then separately they taught his right hand to tear block towers down. On the last day of the experiment they let both the hands work together—the guy actually fought with himself in this film—his left hand tried to build a tower while his right hand constantly wrecked whatever he made. The hands started slapping each other and wrestling with the same block…

The one half of me, see, won't take no for an answer. This me's gonna go out there and take the corporate world by storm, if that's what I decide I want to do, or climb mountains, or pump gas, or write for TV, or…become a stock broker if I happen to feel like it. I do not need male approval to achieve my life goals. Like a fish needs a bicycle, and so on and so on.

But I just can't ignore my pathetic other side—it's so whiny and "needy" inside of me. I yearn for…human touch, God, it's embarrassing, sometimes all I want is to be looked at, admired, soothed and caressed. I still want the power, I still want to make money and go mountaineering. But the thing I want most right now, God, Santa, Gloria Steinem, is some person to love me and sleep in my bed.

First I hate myself for it, then I forgive myself lovingly, then I yell at myself for going soft on myself. Then I cry, usually, and then I get sullen and scowl. Stomp around the place dropping dishes and breaking bric-a-brac. Backlash! I scream, backlash, Sabine! You're contributing to the undeclared war against women! How could you! How dare you! You ought to be shot! Then I usually have a marshmallow sundae to calm myself down.

The saddest thing is, I've got no one to blame. God damn, I wrote my dissertation on this, I know the eight key symptoms and the ten warning signs and the twelve-step recovery program like the back of my hand. How can I be so smart and so stupid?

So I've made a very adult decision. If I can't change the world, I have to change myself. I'm gonna lay on my back and suck up the gas and fall into a deep sleep, and when the prince kisses me I'm gonna wake up and be beautiful. And then I'm gonna flush all my feminist morals down the can and I'm gonna sashay my butt out into the glittering suburban night and I'm gonna get laid, goddamnit. Like my mom used to say—you've made your cake, now you have to eat it. I hear you, Ma. Ain't it the truth.

ALL. *(Quietly:)*
This is the way we bake our cake
bake our cake
bake our cake
This is the way we bake our cake
So early Friday morning.

(A flashbulb pops and RENNIE *is propelled into center.)*

RENNIE. The first picture of me is at my first birthday party. In this one I am screaming with laughter and holding my hands up to show the camera that I am covered with chocolate cake. My face is smeared with it, it is all over the front of my pretty pink dress. Apparently I was quite verbally advanced, and my parents were showing me off when my uncle Jake said, Oh yeah? How smart is she? She's a genius, says my mother, she understands everything. Try it. She'll do anything you say.

So…Rennie, says my uncle Jake, smush that chocolate cake all over your face, sweetheart. Will you do that for me?

And I did it of course because I was just that smart and I ruined my dress and they took a picture of me humiliating myself when I was twelve months old.

(Flashbulb pops.)

This one is my mother's favorite. It's of her and me on one of our mother-daughter days, we're on the steps of the Met looking *very* close and what you don't see is Mother boring her knuckles into the small of my back saying Straighten up, sweetheart, it lengthens your neck. Now glow, come on, glow. We want this one to glow.

For awhile there is an absence of photos—when tummies are no longer little-girl cute. Mother hides me at family gatherings and I seem always to end up behind pieces of furniture. So we have no extant record of the long years of wanting, of wanting and wanting and being denied. Reaching for bread and peanut butter and having Slimfast thrust into my twelve-year-old fist. Mother says No, I am putting my foot down. She is putting her foot down, I see, and I see that to want and demand things is bad.

And when I finally want nothing, nothing at all, when I finally want so little I can barely get up in the morning, my head feels like a ten ton brick on my shoulders, my knees buckle walking from class to class, when I want so little the gentlest sounds scrape my ears and my skin is sore and my hair falls out, finally my mother pulls me out from behind the chaise longue and says This is my daughter Rennie! This is my wonderful, beautiful daughter. Out comes the camera!

(Flashbulb pops.)

The pictures reappear. All the while Mother says Sweetheart, you're beautiful. You really do glow.

(*Flashbulb pops.*)

In this one I am standing outside my own house, in a hideous dress I do not recall choosing, it is blue and it feels like a garbage bag next to my skin. I am wearing a floppy white orchid on my wrist and man, am I glowing. I am really fucking glowing. My smile is about this wide on my face though I don't know what I am smiling about because Andrew Marino has his hand on my back. We haven't even left the house yet, my mother is still snapping pictures and there he is, slinking his hand up my dress. Later we are in the dark and he is breathing so hard he is fogging the windshield and I say to him Andrew. No. No. And he says to me Rennie, you're beautiful. Please Rennie please, will you do it for me? I am saying, No, I am saying, Stop, but he does not hear me, I am not loud enough. I am so—*weak*. I am just…too…weak.

(*Flashbulb pops.*)

In this one my mother is getting remarried. She is a vision in indigo organdy, she looks half her age, her husband's in real estate. But heavens, where's Rennie? Rennie's not in this one. Rennie is wearing an attractive off-white linen pants suit, but she is not in her place at her mother's side because she is in the parish hall kitchen, devouring the three-foot-tall wedding cake meant to serve one hundred and eighty guests. It was just so pristine, floating there, with no one to guard it, no one to witness… I ate and I ate and I ate it all up until there wasn't one crumb left, not a single frosted rosette, and I held that whole cake inside my body, I had it all to myself. And then I threw it all up on the kitchen floor and I walked out the back door into the night.

(RENNIE *runs back to her chair, lights shift.*)

CARLY. I wonder what it'll actually be like.

SABINE. I've researched the procedure, I'll describe it if you want.

CARLY. Thanks but no thanks.

SABINE. You'll be knocked out, you won't feel a thing.

RENNIE. What are you afraid of? It's what we've been waiting for.

(Lights shift, up on CEL *in her corner. During the course of the monologue she moves up center and then progressively further downstage.)*

CEL. It starts with a girl maybe six maybe seven, looking down at herself seeing how—horrible she was! How gross like a monster. She didn't look anything like the other kids from 4-H, they were all skinny as rats from dragging goats through the mud and bending over fields in the blazing hot sun. In summer all kids' legs were scabby—but nobody had marks on them like I did, like Cel, Cel had some scars.

The first one came when I was six. I had split open my knee climbing through barbed wire and mama drove me to the hospital to get the thing stitched up with ugly dark thread, that's how deep it was. But I took those stitches out with scissors when I got home. I told my mama they came out in the bath but I could tell by the way she looked at me sidewise frying the eggs that she didn't believe it. All that summer I worked on my knee and by the time Labor Day rolled around my leg looked like it had been caught in a thresher, maybe.

After that she just seemed to find them, Cel, these cuts in her skin, these holes. They seemed to pop up without her even noticing. Some she put in there herself with the kitchen knives for killing the chickens or shears for the garden or the awl daddy used for punching holes in saddles.

Mama didn't know what to do with her girl. At first she didn't say anything, just folded her arms like so across her chest. What's happened to the backs of your feet she asked. You're picking those cuts of yours apart aren't you? What are you doing to yourself Celie? Why do you want to do such a thing to yourself? So she started buying extra boxes of Band-Aids and leaving them about the house in places she thought I might be likely to come across them. But I wanted to—take myself completely apart. I had dreams of my body parts spread out in the yard for everyone even the neighbors to see.

All the way through high school I did it at night when no one was looking. After my shower, when the skin was still soft. It was my thing to know. Then one day my husband found me on the floor of the bathroom, busted in without knocking... After that he kept watching me, keeping track where I went. I tried to lay still. I forgot things...left them to burn on the stove. My husband paced around and slammed the door on his way out. He accused me of letting the heat out in winter, letting animals in, stray cats and birds.

So I needed a final solution. Get rid of all of the flesh at once. I was poking a roaster chicken full of cloves getting ready for Sunday dinner and I went to light the broiler with a hard wooden match. Then it came to me. My body—I wanted to light it on fire. Hear the fat sizzle into smoke. With all the fat gone I could dance—more than that, I could run and jump and fly maybe even, just me and my bones running naked through the meadows feeling the breeze. It seemed so obvious—why hadn't I thought of this before? I struck one of the matches, stroked it smooth cross the rough edge of the box and I could feel the flame sparking and growing and swallowing the match head. I held it in front of my face. It flickered in my own breath. My thighs would go up first I thought then the rest of me would catch on quick. I lifted my leg and dropped the match onto my pants. For a moment—nothing, then—warm hot my leg started to jump—my skin was on fire! I screamed without meaning to Oh my God! I reeled around to face the counter my hands out in front of me reaching desperate—something, anything! Towel potholder glass of water… In my mind I heard Miss Moser from in front of the black board—stop, drop and roll, she said, if you ever catch fire just stop, drop and…

Later I went to the phone to call 911, shivering, numb. I caught fire, I said calmly into the phone. I was cooking a chicken. It escaped.

> (RENNIE, SABINE, *and* CARLY *come over to* CEL *and touch her one by one. They all look at each other, then, embarrassed, start to return to their chairs.* CARLY *stops them by beginning the candy store chant.* SABINE *joins in, then* RENNIE, *so it sounds like a round. When they hit the "Doctor doctor will I die" line they each continue to chant that until they all say it together, including* CEL.)

ALL. I met my boyfriend at the candy store
He bought me ice cream
He bought me cake
He brought me home with a belly ache
Mama mama I feel sick
Call the doctor quick quick quick
Doctor doctor will I die?

CARLY. Count to five and you'll survive

RENNIE. One.

SABINE. Two.

CEL. Three.

CARLY. Four.

ALL. Five.

>*(They look at each other, then simultaneously take off their gowns and drop them on the floor. In their underwear, they walk together downstage and stand facing the audience. The last few lines are light and full of relief.)*

CARLY. Once upon a time there was a very beautiful woman who hardly ever wanted or asked for anything until one day when she suddenly got—very extremely hungry.

CEL. So she said to her husband, honey, climb over that wall and get me some of them radishes I see growing down there in that garden.

SABINE. But this was no ordinary garden.

CARLY. This was no ordinary woman.

RENNIE. This was no ordinary hunger.

>*(Two beats, lights bump out.)*

End of Play